D0581499

WILD RIDES

Boats

Tick

H46 597 055 0

An Hachette UK Company
www.hachette.co.uk

First published in Great Britain in 2012 by
TickTock, a division of Octopus Publishing Group Ltd
Endeavour House
189 Shaftesbury Avenue
London
WC2H 8JY
www.octopusbooks.co.uk

Copyright © Octopus Publishing Group Ltd 2012

All rights reserved. No part of this work may be reproduced or utilised in any form or by any means, electronic or mechanical, including photocopying, recording or by any information storage and retrieval system, without the prior written permission of the publisher.

ISBN 978 1 84898 633 6

A CIP catalogue record for this book is available from the British Library

Printed and bound in China

10 9 8 7 6 5 4 3 2 1

Picture credits:
b=bottom; c=center; t=top; r=right; l=left
Alamy: p.6-7 all, p.21t, p.25t. Beken of Cowes: p.12-13c, p.18-19c. British Antarctic Survey: p.14-15 all. Corbis: p.8-9c, p.16-17 all, p.19t, p.20-21c. Hawkes Ocean Technologies: p.9t. John Clark Photography: p.4-5c. RNLI: p.28-29 all. Stena: p.24c. World of Residensea: p. 26-27 all. Yamaha: p.1, p.26-27 all.

Every effort has been made to trace the copyright holders, and we apologise in advance for any unintentional omissions. We would be pleased to insert the appropriate acknowledgments in any subsequent edition of this publication.

Contents

California Quake Drag Boat

The fastest racing boats on the water are drag boats. These single-seater crafts surge like rockets at breathtaking speeds over the waves, often spending more time above the surface than on it.

Thanks to the 5,000 hp engine, this drag boat became the first to achieve ¼ mile in under 5 seconds - a world record!

Bottled air is supplied to the driver's helmet. If the driver crashes, he can still breathe while waiting for divers to rescue him.

DID YOU KNOW?

This model has reached speeds of 370 km/h (230 mph).

The safety capsule breaks free from the boat in the event of a high-speed crash.

STATS & FACTS

LAUNCHED: 1999

ORIGIN: US

ENGINES: 8194 CUBIC CM NITROMETHANE ENGINE GENERATING 5,000 HP

LENGTH: 7.62 M

WIDTH: 3.72 M

MAXIMUM SPEED: 198 KNOTS (370 KM/H / 230 MPH)

MAXIMUM WEIGHT: 4.75 TONNES

LOAD: 1 PILOT

FUEL CAPACITY: 20 LITRES

COST: £60,000

June Hong Chian Lee Chinese Junk

The junk is an ancient Chinese sailing vessel that first sailed over 2,000 years ago. It was used for trading goods throughout Asia. The *June Hong Chian Lee* is a traditional teak-wood merchant vessel that was renovated and is now a luxury boat for tourists. It has six cabins.

The hull is divided into compartments called bulkheads. If water leaks into one it cannot spread to the others, so the ship stays afloat.

DID YOU KNOW?

Junk doesn't mean rubbish. It comes from a Chinese word for boat.

Nicknamed 'The Junk', the *June Hong Chian Lee* has engines, showers, satellite navigation and air-conditioning.

Linen sails are held together by a wooden frame.

STATS & FACTS

LAUNCHED: 1962

REBUILT: 1997

ORIGIN: THAILAND

ENGINES: ONE MAIN ENGINE THAT GENERATES 380 HP

LENGTH: 33 M

WIDTH: 8.5 M

MAXIMUM SPEED: 8 KNOTS (15 KM/H / 9.2 MPH)

MAXIMUM WEIGHT: 5.4 TONNES

LOAD: 18 PASSENGERS, CREW OF 10

FUEL CAPACITY: 10,000 LITRES

COST: £1.2 MILLION

Deep Flight Submersible

Submersibles are miniature submarines used for deep-sea exploration. *Deep Flight* is a tiny one-person submersible with short wings that allow it to 'fly' through the water.

Lightweight material is strong enough to resist the tremendous pressure of the deep.

DID YOU KNOW?

In 2012, filmmaker and ocean explorer James Cameron reached the deepest point in the ocean – the Mariana Trench – in a custom-built one-man submersible. He descended almost 11 km (7 miles).

A submersible has the layout of a plane. Unlike a plane, however, the stubby wings pull the craft down through the water, rather than up off the ground.

Deep Flight is equipped with six lights, which are needed because the bottom of the ocean is totally dark.

STATS & FACTS

LAUNCHED: 1996

ORIGIN: US

ENGINES: TWO MOTORS POWERED BY TEN 12-VOLT, LEAD-ACID BATTERIES, GENERATING 5 HP EACH

LENGTH: 4 M

WIDTH: 2.4 M

MAXIMUM SPEED: 12 KNOTS (22.2 KM/H / 13.8 MPH)

MAXIMUM WEIGHT: 3 TONNES

ASCENT RATE: 198 M PER MINUTE

DESCENT RATE: 150 M PER MINUTE

MAXIMUM DEPTH: NEWER *DEEP FLIGHT CHALLENGER* WILL REACH 11 KM

LOAD: 1 PILOT

COST: £1 MILLION (IN 2009)

Endeavour Ship-Rigged Bark

Today, travelling around the world takes just two days. In 1768, it took Captain James Cook three years to make the journey in his ship *Endeavour*. In 1994, a replica of the vessel duplicated the voyage of the original craft.

The small triangular sail at the front is called the jib, while the highest one on the middle mast is the main topgallant.

DID YOU KNOW?

The original *Endeavour* began life as a coal-carrier and ended up as a French whaling ship.

Ordinary sailors slept in hammocks hung 35 cm apart. The captain's cabin had sash windows, a table and stove, fine furniture, books and paintings.

Extra planks on the hull slow down the damage caused by shipworms, which feed on wood.

STATS & FACTS

LAUNCHED: 1993

ORIGIN: AUSTRALIA

ENGINES: TWO 6-CYLINDER CATERPILLAR DIESELS GENERATING 405 HP

LENGTH: 42 M

WIDTH: 9.8 M

HEIGHT TO TOP MAST: 30 M

MAXIMUM SPEED: 8 KNOTS (15 KM/H / 9.2 MPH)

MAXIMUM WEIGHT: 397 TONNES

LOAD: 16 PERMANENT CREW, 36 VOYAGE CREW AND 4 OTHER

FUEL CAPACITY: 132,500 LITRES

COST: £6 MILLION

Illbruck Racing Yacht

Inspired by the Whitbread Round the World Race and called the 'Everest of sailing', the Volvo Ocean Race has taken place every three years since 2001. The nine-month race covers 59,500 km (37,000 miles). The first winner was *Illbrook Challenge*.

Crews pull the cables for the sails using high-speed winches with long handles. The tallest mast is 26 m.

DID YOU KNOW?

The original race was inspired by the great seafarers who sailed the world's oceans aboard square-rigged clipper ships more than a century ago.

Round-the-world yachts battle giant waves, howling gales, collisions with icebergs and whales – and each other!

The satellite communications centre contains telephone, email and video transmission facilities.

STATS & FACTS

LAUNCHED: 2001

ORIGIN: GERMANY

ENGINES: N/A

LENGTH: 19.5 M

WIDTH: 5.25 M

MAXIMUM SPEED: 36.75 KNOTS (67.6 KM/H / 42 MPH)

MAXIMUM WEIGHT: 13.5 TONNES

LOAD: 12 PEOPLE

COST: £16 MILLION

James Clark Ross Research Ship

One of the world's toughest ships, the RRS *James Clark Ross* can steam through sea ice over 1 m thick. The vessel is a huge floating laboratory, used for exploring and performing scientific research in the freezing waters of Antarctica.

The main hull is made of extra-thick steel, which helps the ship move through thick ice.

The ship surveys the oceans and measures depths and currents. It also acts as a floating weather station and even searches for strange creatures of the deep.

DID YOU KNOW?

A compressed air system prevents ice from squeezing and cracking the hull by rolling the ship from side to side.

There are five main laboratories and science rooms on board. More can be loaded onto the deck in house-sized containers.

LAUNCHED: 1990

ORIGIN: UNITED KINGDOM

ENGINES: TWO X WARTSILA R32 (3.1 MW EACH) AND TWO X WARTSILA R22 (1.0 MW) ENGINES DELIVERING 8,500 HP

LENGTH: 99 M

WIDTH: 18.85 M

MAXIMUM SPEED: 15.7 KNOTS (30 KM/H / 18 MPH)

MAXIMUM WEIGHT: 7,767 TONNES LOADED

LOAD: 12 OFFICERS, 15 CREW, 1 DOCTOR, 31 SCIENTISTS (MAXIMUM)

FUEL CAPACITY: 1,350 CUBIC M

COST: £37.5 MILLION

Los Angeles Fireboat No. 2

Although ships are surrounded by water, they sometimes catch fire. Their engines and fuel may go up in flames, or they might carry a cargo like oil that can burn. Almost every big port has fireboats on hand to tackle emergencies. This vessel belongs to the Los Angeles Fire Department.

DID YOU KNOW?

Firefighters wear breathing gear for protection. Some poisonous smoke can kill in just a few seconds.

2 LOS ANGELES CITY FIRE

The fireboats put out electrical blazes by spraying special foam instead of water.

All parts of the fireboat are flameproof, in case there is an explosion of burning fuel nearby.

The fireboat has a fully equipped emergency room where paramedics work on casualties, a retractable diving platform, a telescopic aerial ladder and underwater cameras.

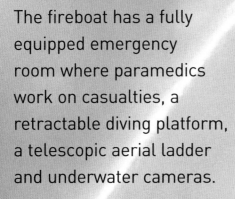

STATS & FACTS

LAUNCHED: 1925 (UPDATED LATE 1960S)

ORIGIN: US

ENGINES: TWO 700 HP V-12 CUMMINS; THREE 380 HP 6-CYLINDER IN-LINE CUMMINS; AND TWO 525 HP V-12 2-CYCLE DETROITS, PLUS SIX ENGINES FOR PUMPS

LENGTH: 30 M

WIDTH: 6 M

MAXIMUM SPEED: 17 KNOTS (31.5 KM/H / 19.6 MPH)

MAXIMUM WEIGHT: 152 TONNES

LOAD: 14 CREW

FUEL CAPACITY: 9,801 LITRES

COST: £135,550 (IN 1925)

Nimitz-Class Aircraft Carrier

Nimitz-class aircraft carriers are the biggest warships ever built. Each of these giants is a floating army, navy and air force. The crew is the size of a small town: 3,360 ship's crew and 2,500 air crew, not including soldiers and pilots!

The supercarrier holds up to 85 planes and six helicopters, along with their crew and supplies. Jet fuel is stored in swimming-pool-sized tanks.

DID YOU KNOW?

These nuclear-powered ships can go 20 years without refuelling and have a life span of 50 years.

Supercarriers are equipped with the latest computers, radar and missiles. It takes three years to refuel, re-equip and refit these monsters.

The *Nimitz*-class supercarrier is almost as long as the Empire State Building is tall.

STATS & FACTS

LAUNCHED: 1972

ORIGIN: US

ENGINES: TWO NUCLEAR ENGINES POWERING 4 STEAM TURBINES PRODUCING 260,000 HP

LENGTH: 333 M

WIDTH: 40.8 M

MAXIMUM SPEED: MORE THAN 30 KNOTS (56 KM/H / 35 MPH)

MAXIMUM WEIGHT: 100,000 TONNES

LOAD: 3,360 SHIP'S COMPANY AND 2,500 AIR CREW

COST: £1.25 BILLION

Jahre Viking Oil Supertanker

The largest ships in the world are giant tankers that carry crude oil. Their precious cargo is used to make everything from petrol to paint and plastic. The biggest one started life as the *Seawise Giant*. It was later known as the *Happy Giant*, *Jahre Viking*, *Knock Nevis* and *Mont*, before it was retired in 2010. It was so big it took 8 km (5 miles) to come to a stop!

DID YOU KNOW?

The ship was too big to navigate the English Channel, the Suez Canal and the Panama Canal.

Oil was pumped on board through pipes at an oil rig and off again at a refinery.

Most of the ship was controlled by computer. Only 33 crew members were needed.

The deck area was as large as four football pitches. Crew members sometimes used bicycles to get around!

STATS & FACTS

LAUNCHED: 1979

ORIGIN: JAPAN

ENGINES: FOUR STEAM TURBINES (37,300 KW) GENERATING 50,019 HP EACH

LENGTH: 458 M

WIDTH: 69 M

MAXIMUM SPEED: 10 KNOTS (18.5 KM/H / 11.5 MPH)

MAXIMUM WEIGHT: 647,955 TONNES FULLY LOADED

CREW: 35 TO 40 PEOPLE

LOAD: 4,240,865 BARRELS OF OIL

FUEL CAPACITY: 20,000 LITRES

Yamaha FZR WaveRunner

A combination of motorcycle, water ski and snow mobile, the WaveRunner can surge across waves at great speeds. It was the first sit-down watercraft designed for stand-up riding.

Thanks to nanotechnology, the WaveRunner has stronger hulls, decks and liners that are 25 per cent lighter than previous models.

DID YOU KNOW?

The telescopic steering column makes it easy for riders to go from sitting to standing, with three different riding positions.

Riders perform amazing turns, jumps and loops. They can even dive completely under the water!

The keel shape is designed for high-speed, supertight turning. Large pump inlet ducts provide great pickup.

STATS & FACTS

LAUNCHED: 2009

ORIGIN: US

ENGINE: 4-CYLINDER, 4-STROKE

LENGTH: 3.4 M

WIDTH: 1.23 M

SPEED: 0 TO 50 KM (30 MPM) IN 1.7 SECONDS

MAXIMUM WEIGHT: 160 KG

LOAD: 2 RIDERS

FUEL CAPACITY: 70 LITRES

COST: UP TO £8,000

Stena Discovery HSS Ferry

Stena HSS ferries (High-speed Sea Service) are high-speed car carriers. They are catamarans, which means they have two hulls instead of one. The design makes for a smooth, speedy ride.

DID YOU KNOW?

Most car ferries are 'Ro-Ro' – roll (drive) on and roll (drive) off. In the past, cranes lifted each car on and off the boats.

The hulls are made from aluminium, which is light and does not rust.

Ferries operate worldwide. This one serves the Caribbean and can hold 200 cars and 1,000 passengers. It has lounge areas where passengers can relax during the crossing.

Four massive gas turbine engines produce as much power as 600 car engines.

STATS & FACTS

LAUNCHED: 1997

ORIGIN: FINLAND

ENGINES: TWO GE LM2500 GAS TURBINES, GENERATING 20,500 KW (27,490 HP) EACH, AND TWO GE LM1600 GAS TURBINES, PRODUCING 13,500 KW (18,103 HP) EACH

LENGTH: 126.5 M

WIDTH: 40 M

MAXIMUM SPEED: 40 KNOTS (74 KM/H / 46 MPH)

MAXIMUM WEIGHT: 1,500 TONNES

LOAD: 1,500 PASSENGERS AND 375 CARS

FUEL CAPACITY: 10,000 LITRES

COST: £65 MILLION

The World Luxury Liner

The World is a luxury liner with a difference - its passengers live on it! For a vast price, residents buy a set of rooms that they call home. The ship travels around the world to exciting events, including the Rio de Janeiro Carnival in Brazil and the Formula 1 Motor Race in Monaco.

The hull is made of giant pieces of steel, lifted into place by powerful cranes.

DID YOU KNOW?

The ship houses an art gallery, a florist and 12,000 bottles of champagne.

On *The World* people are not passengers, but residents on a lifetime vacation.

The 12 decks offer every luxury imaginable: restaurants, a casino, a nightclub, theatres, gyms, tennis courts, swimming pools and cinemas.

STATS & FACTS

LAUNCHED: 2001

ORIGIN: NORWAY

ENGINES: TWO WARTSILA 12 CYLINDER DIESELS, GENERATING 5520 KW (7402 HP)

LENGTH: 196.35 M

WIDTH: 29.8 M

MAXIMUM SPEED: 18.5 KNOTS (34 KM/H / 21 MPH)

MAXIMUM WEIGHT: 43,524 TONNES

LOAD: MAXIMUM OF 976 RESIDENTS, GUESTS AND CREW

FUEL CAPACITY: 1,150 CUBIC M

COST: £164 MILLION

Trent-Type Lifeboat

Every sailor fears shipwreck and drowning at sea. Brave lifeboat crews are always ready for rescue missions, even in the worst storms. Powerful Trent-type lifeboats are run by Britain's RNLI (Royal National Lifeboat Institution).

The survivor's cabin holds ten people. On board there are also heaters, dry clothes and a small galley.

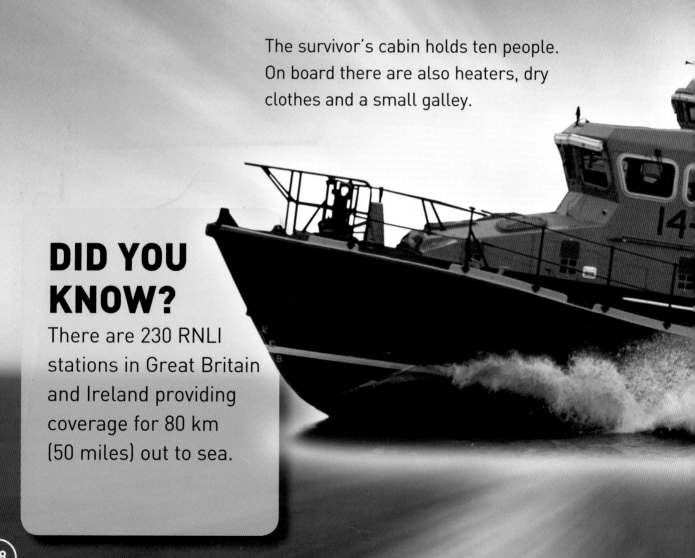

DID YOU KNOW?

There are 230 RNLI stations in Great Britain and Ireland providing coverage for 80 km (50 miles) out to sea.

Radar and radio equipment track ships in distress using the Marsat and Sarsat emergency satellite navigation systems.

The hull is made of plastic, carbon fibre and composites. These materials are light, strong and never rust.

STATS & FACTS

LAUNCHED: 1994

ORIGIN: UNITED KINGDOM

ENGINES: TWO-MAN DIESELS, 808 HP PER ENGINE, EACH ABOUT AS POWERFUL AS A FORMULA 1 RACING CAR ENGINE

LENGTH: 14.26 M

MAXIMUM SPEED: 25 KNOTS (47 KM/H / 29 MPH)

MAXIMUM WEIGHT: 27.5 TONNES

LOAD: 6 CREW, PLUS 10 SURVIVORS

FUEL CAPACITY: 4,100 LITRES

COST: £1.2 MILLION

Glossary

ALUMINIUM A lightweight, strong metal that does not rust.

BARK Another name for a ship.

BRIDGE A ship's main control room from where it is steered. It is usually situated high up to provide good views in all directions.

BULKHEADS Dividing 'walls' that run across the inside of a ship, from side to side. They have doors for people to pass through.

CABIN A room or enclosed area on a ship or boat.

CARBON FIBRE A modern, lightweight material used to make many vehicles.

CATAMARAN A boat or ship with two hulls that are joined together by a wide deck or decks over the top.

COMPOSITE A material or substance that is made of a mixture of materials, such as plastic, metal and fibreglass. Composites are usually very light and strong.

DECKS The main floors or stories of a ship and especially the uppermost flat area where people walk.

ENGINE The part of a vehicle where fuel is burned to create energy.

GALLEY The kitchen or dining area on a ship.

HULL The main part or body of a ship that floats on the water.

HORSEPOWER (HP) The measure of an engine's power, originally based on the power of an engine compared to a horse.

JET Stream of fluid forced out under pressure from a narrow opening or nozzle.

JIB A triangular sail usually at the front of a yacht or sailing ship.

KNOT One nautical mile per hour, equivalent to 1.15 miles per hour or 1.85 kilometres per hour.

LINEN Durable material often used to make a ship's sails.

LINER A large ship that carries passengers.

LABORATORY Somewhere equipped for scientific experimentation or research.

MAST A tall pole on a ship that may hold up sails, radio antennas, radar dishes or even flags.

NANOTECHNOLOGY The science of using materials on a molecular scale, especially to create microscopic devices.

PUMP A machine used for raising water or other liquids.

RADAR A system using invisible radio waves that are beamed out and reflected back by objects as 'echoes'. These are displayed on a screen to help identify other ships, planes, land, icebergs and similar items.

REFINERY Place where oil is turned into petrol.

RIGGED A ship equipped with sails and the ropes and chains used to control them.

ROLL CAGE A metal framework within some racing boats that prevents crushing in the event that the boat turns over in a crash.

RUDDER A large, wide, flat part of the boat that can be tilted from side to side for steering. Usually situated at the rear, or stern, of a ship.

SAILS Fabric spread to catch or deflect the wind as a means of propelling a ship or boat.

STEEL Very strong alloy usually made by combining iron with carbon.

STERN The rear part of a ship or boat.

SATELLITE NAVIGATION A system that tells you where you are by using satellites in space.

SUBMERSIBLE A boat that can function when under water.

TOPGALLANT The top part of a ship's mast.

WINCHES System that lifts something by winding a line around a spool.

Index